MICHAEL FARADAY
and the
Modern World

Brian Bowers
PhD, C.Eng, MIEE

Published by E·P·A Press, Wendens Ambo, Essex

Published by EPA Press, Wendens Ambo, UK.

© 1991 Brian Bowers

Additional copies of this book should be available through any good bookshop. In case of difficulty please contact the publishers directly at

E P A Press
Blythburgh House
Wendens Ambo
Saffron Walden
Essex, CB11 4JU

British Library Cataloguing in Publication Data

Bowers, Brian
  Michael Faraday and the modern world.
  1. Physics. Faraday Michael 1791-1867
  I. Title
  530.92
  ISBN 0-9517362-0-5

Printed in Singapore at Stamford Press Pte Ltd.

CONTENTS

Michael Faraday
from a lithograph by T H Maguire, 1851

INTRODUCTION

Ours is an electric world. We all use electric lights. We all use electric motors at home (think of the tape recorder, food mixer, vacuum cleaner, refrigerator, fan heater, ...). We all listen to the radio and watch television. Industry uses electric motors to drive its machines - this book was printed on an electrically driven press. We travel on electric trains. Even our cars have electric starters.

A world without electricity is now almost inconceivable. The basic ideas behind electricity *generation* and many of the *applications* of electricity, as well as the first idea of *electromagnetic waves* ('*radio*' *waves*), have their origins in the work of Michael Faraday.

He is sometimes called 'the father of electricity', though perhaps a better description was Sir William Bragg's phrase 'the man who made electrical engineering possible'. Faraday was both a *scientific investigator* and an *explainer* of science. An early desire for a career in science led him to a job as Laboratory Assistant at the Royal Institution in London. There he was able to carry out fundamental research in chemistry and electricity and present his discoveries in lectures and publications. His lectures proved very popular; Charles Dickens said of them in his *Household Words* 'You should go and hear him yourself'. Best known of Faraday's lectures were the Royal Institution Christmas Lectures for Young People. Faraday instituted them, and they are still given every year.

This book is about Michael Faraday, his life, his work, and some of the many things we take for granted in modern life which owe their origins to him. It was published to accompany an exhibition on the same theme at the Science Museum marking the bicentenary of Faraday's birth. The exhibition was sponsored by London Electricity, and much assistance was given also by the Royal Institution and the Institution of Electrical Engineers. I gratefully acknowledge the assistance of both those bodies, and the help of many friends and colleagues including Eryl Davies, J V Field, David Gooding, Frank James, Irene McCabe, Katie Petty-Saphon, Lenore Symons, John Thomas, Peter Turvey and David Woodcock.

Brian Bowers

Sunday Afternoon
July 12th 1812

Dear A

      I have lately made a few simple galvanic experiments merely to illustrate to my self the first principles of the science. I was going to Knights ... [and bought some zinc] ... I obtained it for the purpose of forming discs, with which & copper to make a little battery, the first I completed contained the immense number of seven pair of Plates!!! and of the immense size of half-pence each!!! I, Sir, my own self, cut out seven discs of the size of half-pennies each! I, Sir, covered them with seven half-pence and I interposed between seven or rather six pieces of paper, soaked in a solution of muriate of Soda!!! - but laugh no longer Dear A--- rather wonder at the effects this trivial power produced, it was sufficient to produce the decomposition of the Sulphate of Magnesia; an effect which extremely surprised me, for I did not - could not have any Idea, that the agent was competent to the purpose. ... My proof that the Sulphate was decomposed, was, that in about 2 hours the clear solution became turbid, Magnesia was suspended in it.

I am dear A----
Yours Sincerely
M Faraday

Letter from Faraday to Benjamin Abbott, describing his first electrical experiment.

EARLY LIFE

Michael Faraday was a blacksmith's son, who became the greatest scientific discoverer of his time and also the greatest explainer of science to the public.

The Surrey village of Newington, where he was born on 22 September 1791, is now part of London. Michael was the third child of James and Margaret Faraday who had recently moved south from Westmorland. He had an elder sister, Elizabeth, born in 1787, and a brother, Robert, born in 1788. The family soon moved again, north of the River Thames, and lived at first in rooms over a coach house in Jacob's Well Mews, Manchester Square. Here another sister, Margaret, was born in 1802. Michael Faraday's early years were hard, and he had little formal education. In later life he said: 'My education was of the most ordinary description, consisting of little more than the rudiments of reading, writing, and arithmetic at a common day school. My hours out of school were passed at home and in the streets.'

In 1804 Michael went to work as an errand boy for George Riebau, a bookseller and bookbinder whose premises were nearby in Blandford Street. One of his duties was to deliver newspapers, and in some cases to collect them back. In those days, many people could not afford to buy a newspaper, and so paid to read one which had to be returned. The following year, when he was fourteen, Michael was apprenticed to

1 Riebau's shop.

Riebau as a bookbinder and bookseller. In 1809 his parents moved again, to Weymouth Street, where his father died in October 1810. Although Michael was

3

then living at Riebau's, it is clear from subsequent correspondence that he regarded the Weymouth Street address as home.

Nothing is known about Faraday's life in the first few years of his apprenticeship, but he became a competent bookbinder and some volumes bound by him are still in existence. This practical training in working with his hands stood him in good stead in later years, when great skill with laboratory apparatus was vital to his scientific work. He read many of the books which he bound and became interested in science, especially chemistry and electricity, which he read about in the *Encyclopaedia Britannica*. Riebau encouraged his interests, and in

2 Frictional electric machine believed to be the one made by Faraday when an apprentice.

his spare time Faraday repeated some of the experiments he had read about. He built a frictional electric machine which is still preserved at the Royal Institution in London.

Walking in the City of London one day, he saw an advertisement for a series of evening lectures on 'natural philosophy' (the nineteenth-century term for pure science). The lectures were given by a Mr Tatum who led a group called The City Philosophical Society. The meetings were held in his house on Wednesday evenings. Tatum gave a scientific lecture with demonstrations every two weeks; alternate Wednesdays one of the other members would speak. Faraday joined the Society with a shilling fee paid by his brother, Robert, who was by then a working blacksmith.

The City Philosophical Society was effectively a secondary school for Faraday. During the years 1810 and 1811, he heard lectures on all kinds of subjects - chemistry, electricity, hydrostatics, optics, mechanics, geology, astronomy. Here also he met Benjamin Abbott, a young Quaker who worked in the City. The two became close friends. Much of our knowledge of this part of Faraday's life comes from his letters to Abbott, which still survive, and from some notes written by Abbott after Faraday's death.

In one of these letters [part of which is reproduced on page 2] he describes making a Voltaic pile - a simple battery using copper coins, some pieces of zinc, and paper soaked in salt water. The letter conveys something of the excitement Faraday felt in his first electrical experiments, and also the patience he brought to his researches. There were no meters to show that his pile was producing electricity, and he had to wait two hours for the electrochemical effect to become visible.

Faraday took detailed notes of Tatum's lectures and later wrote them out in full, sometimes noting that he disagreed with Tatum about something. On one occasion he made his disagreement known in the discussion after the lecture, and was then invited to address the Society. The point in dispute was the nature of electricity. Most scientists thought that electricity was an 'imponderable fluid' (a fluid having no weight) which could pass through solid objects. (Heat and magnetism were explained in a similar way). The question was: were there two electric fluids, one positive and one negative? Or was there a single fluid?

Tatum thought electric effects were caused by a single fluid which was always present in some quantity. Too much produced a positive charge, and too little a negative one. Faraday's lecture, which was written out in full, sets out the arguments for there being two electric fluids. This was the first talk in public given by the man who was to become the greatest scientific lecturer of his time.

One of Riebau's customers, a Mr Dance, was impressed with Faraday's interest in science. He gave him tickets to hear Sir Humphry Davy lecturing at the Royal Institution. Following his practice at the City Philosophical Society, Faraday took detailed notes, which he bound himself. Later he was to send the bound volume to Davy with a letter asking for a job in any scientific capacity.

Throughout his life Faraday kept a series of 'common place books' or notebooks in which he jotted down facts, quotations, ideas and questions as they came to him. One note, written in 1822, explains the value of such books: 'I already owe much to these notes, and think such a collection worth the making by every scientific man. I am sure none would think the trouble lost after a year's experience.'

The earliest one, now in the Archives of the Institution of Electrical Engineers in London, is described on its first page as: 'A collection of Notices, Occurrences, Events, etc., relating to the Arts and Sciences, collected from the Public Papers, Reviews, Magazines, and other miscellaneous works. Intended to promote both Amusement and Instruction and also to corroborate or invalidate those theories which are continually starting in the world of science.'

The notes tell us something of the range of Faraday's interests and his sense of humour. He quotes the *Liverpool Courier* of 1823:

Walking the streets. - It has been found a difficult thing at Liverpool to make the townsfolk adopt the well-known and useful rule of keeping the right-hand side of the path in walking; and reason having failed, an attempt has been made to shame them into obedience to it, the following courteous placard having appeared on the walls of the town: "Respectable people are requested to keep the right-hand side of the footpath and Blackguards the left".

Press cutting in Faraday's Common Place Book

There is also a recipe for making gin which is reproduced here with some hesitation because although Faraday headed the page 'Excellent Gin' he added afterwards: 'I suspect ..... that there is some mistake in the quantities'!

Receipt to make Gin.

Pearl Ashes	¼ ℔
Pot Ashes	do
Spirit Lye water	3 Quarts
Oil of vitriol	1 oz
Oil of Almonds	1 Pint
Lime water	1 Gallon
Lump sugar	1 ℔
Spirit of Wine	1 Pint
Turpentine	¼ oz

NB. Mix the oils with the spirits of wine to kill them.

For the Lime water — 8 ℔ of unslaked lime; put it into a pail and pour on it 3 quarts of soft water: 1 hour, add three gallons and a quart of water: let it stand for 24 hours clear it off and ork it up for use.

The above receipt and directions were given to me, as correct, for the making of excellent gin. I suspect, nevertheless, that there is some mistake in the quantities; as of the Oil of Almonds. &c.

3 A page from one of Faraday's Common Place Books.

ELECTRICITY BEFORE FARADAY

When Faraday became interested in electricity the word usually meant what we now call 'static' electricity. It had long been known that when dry amber or glass is rubbed it can attract small pieces of paper, and that combing the hair on a cold, dry day sometimes produces sparks. A crackle of tiny electrical discharges can often be heard from clothes made of synthetic fibres, especially as they are removed from a drier. The friction of the feet when walking across a carpet can build up enough electric charge on the body to cause a shock on touching a large metal object, or another person.

Static electricity was studied by the American statesman and scientist Benjamin Franklin. He was the first to distinguish between conductors and insulators, and he introduced the terms 'positive' and 'negative'. His best known research was a very dangerous experiment in which he flew a kite in a thunder storm and showed that electric charges were conducted down the wet string from the lightning clouds. Probably he did not realise how dangerous it was, but at least one other experimenter was killed trying to do the same thing.

The illustrations below are from a long article in the *Encyclopaedia Britannica* which Faraday read. They show a frictional electric machine, a 'battery' of Leyden jars for storing electric charge, and things for demonstrating what static electricity can do.

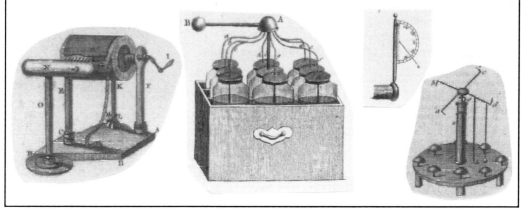

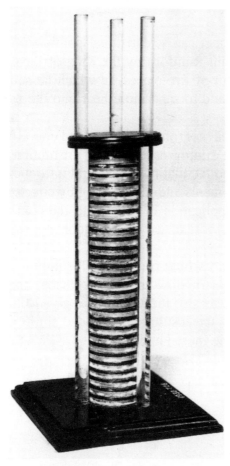

Alessandro Volta described his 'pile', the first apparatus for producing a continuous current of electricity, in 1800. The description came in a long letter written in French to Sir Joseph Banks, President of the Royal Society of London. The pile ('colonne' in French) consisted of thirty or more pieces of two different metals, such as copper and silver, arranged alternately. Between each pair of metals was a piece of card or leather soaked in salt water (so the order was silver - card - copper - silver - card - copper etc). The result, said Volta, was apparatus having the properties of Leyden jars but which acted continuously.

In London Anthony Carlisle, a surgeon, and William Nicholson, a chemist, made a pile according to Volta's description and found that they could use it to decompose water into its elements. The discovery prompted others to make 'batteries', as we now call them, and investigate the effects of continuous currents of electricity.

The first mass-produced battery based on Volta's work was designed by William Cruickshank. He had copper and zinc plates soldered together in pairs and then sealed with wax in grooves in a wooden trough (see illustration on page 29). This arrangement formed a number of compartments which were filled with acid. Faraday used Cruickshank batteries for many of his early electrical experiments at the Royal Institution, and they were the main source of electricity until the Daniell cell was invented in 1836.

THE ROYAL INSTITUTION

Benjamin Thompson (1753-1814) was an American scientist and politician. He travelled widely and was given the title Count Rumford by the King of Bavaria. He is best known for his work on the design of fire-places, in which he sought to solve the problem of smoking chimneys and to send more heat into the room rather than up the chimney.

While living in London, Rumford led a group who founded the Royal Institution of Great Britain (usually known simply as the Royal Institution) in March 1799. It was created 'for diffusing and facilitating the general introduction of useful mechanical inventions and improvements and for teaching by courses of philosphical lectures and experiments the application of science to the common purposes of life'. It has been described as a sort of technical school, but that is not an adequate description.

The founders hoped that wealthy patrons would finance the Institution, and that the working classes would attend to learn how to apply science 'to the common purposes of life' in their work. It was also the intention to give lectures which interested the upper classes, and since the Institution depended entirely on their money the lectures for them became the most important.

Sir Humphry Davy (1778-1829), a Cornish surgeon and chemist, became lecturer in chemistry and geology at the Royal Institution in 1801 and was appointed Professor in the following year. He was a brilliant speaker. His courses on such subjects as agricultural chemistry or the art of tanning drew the fashionable society of London. They may sound mundane subjects to us, but the Managers of the Royal Institution chose them because they wanted to encourage the use of science in farming and business. Davy's eloquence helped to save the Institution from

4 Sir Humphry Davy.

bankruptcy and the reputation he gained from his chemical discoveries helped that of the Institution.

During his first years at the Royal Institution, Davy worked on chemistry and electricity. He obtained for the first time the metals potassium, sodium, calcium, strontium, barium and magnesium by using electricity to decompose their oxides. In 1808 he received the Napoleon prize of 3,000 francs for his electrical researches, despite the fact that Britain and France were at war. In 1812 he was knighted by the Prince Regent, and he was made a baronet in 1818. He is best known for his invention in 1815 of the miner's safety lamp. Davy also tried to break down chlorine without success and concluded it must be an element. This was the man whom Faraday heard lecturing on chemistry four times in 1812.

5 Alessandro Volta demonstrating his 'pile' to Napoleon, who was very interested in science.

On 7 October 1812, Faraday's apprenticeship with George Riebau was completed. He began work as a journeyman bookbinder for a Mr De La Roche, who seems to have been a difficult master. Faraday began to consider seriously whether he might find a career in science. He wrote to Sir Joseph Banks, the President of the Royal Society, asking for a scientific job, but received no reply. Later in October 1812, however, Davy was temporarily blinded by an explosion in the laboratory. Faraday was introduced to Davy - possibly by Mr Dance - and worked for Davy for a few days as a secretary.

After this Faraday wrote to Davy asking for a scientific post, and sending the volume he had made of Davy's lectures. There was no vacancy at the time, but in February 1813 the laboratory assistant, William Payne, who had been employed by the Royal Institution for some ten years, was dismissed for getting into a fight with the instrument maker, John Newman. Davy promptly sent for Faraday and offered him the job. The Managers of the Royal Institution formally agreed, on 1 March 1813, that 'Michael Faraday be engaged to fill the situation lately occupied by Mr Payne on the same terms.' The duties of the Laboratory Assistant had been stated formally by the Managers of the Royal Institution only a few weeks previously. Possibly that was done because of some dispute about what exactly Newman was expected to do. Whatever the reason, it gives us a clear statement of the duties with which Faraday began his scientific career. The Assistant was required:

---

to attend and assist the Lecturers and Professors in preparing for and during their Lectures where any Instruments or Apparatus may be required. To attend to their careful removal from the Model-room and Laboratory to the Lecture room and to clean and replace them after being used, reporting to the Managers such accidents as shall require repair. A constant diary being kept by him for that purpose. That one day in each week he be employed in keeping clean the models in the Repository. And that all the models in the Glass cases be cleaned and dusted at least once within the month.

The Laboratory Assistant's duties at the Royal Institution.

Although he was only a laboratory assistant, Faraday's abilities were quickly recognised. His first work was preparing various substances in the laboratory, but he was soon helping with demonstrations at the various lectures given in the Institution.

Faraday had never been abroad and in fact he had never travelled more than twelve miles from London. Sir Humphry Davy had made occasional tours in the British Isles collecting mineral specimens for the Royal Institution, and he had taken William Payne with him. In 1813 Davy resigned his Professorship (though he was then made Honorary Professor of Chemistry) to make a tour of Europe, and invited Faraday to go with him.

EUROPEAN TOUR

The sons of upper class English families had traditionally finished their education by going on the 'Grand Tour' of Europe with their tutors. It was not an experience that a blacksmith's son could have expected at any time, and all such travels were normally impossible during the wars with France. Napoleon, however, had given special permission for Davy to travel through France and Italy on scientific business. Davy's principal objective was to study the chemistry of volcanic lavas.

The idea of making the tour at that time must have seemed foolish to many people, and the visit attracted some criticism in the British press as unpatriotic, but Davy went. The tour eventually lasted eighteen months, and while they were away Faraday learned French and Italian. He met many of the leading scientists of France, Switzerland and Italy, and discussed their work with them.

Sir Humphry and Lady Davy, with Faraday and Lady Davy's maid, left London on Wednesday, 13 October 1813. Davy's valet, La Fontaine, had also been going to accompany the party, but at the last minute he refused to go and Davy asked Faraday to act as valet also until they arrived in Paris where he would engage another. In the event they never found another valet and Faraday continued the 'temporary' extra duties. There were personal difficulties on the way, since Lady Davy insisted on treating Faraday as a servant, although Sir Humphry was looking on him more and more as a scientific colleague.

They travelled first to Plymouth. Faraday kept a *Journal* in which he recorded his wonder at the scenery, especially in Devon, which was so unlike anything he had seen around London. On the Friday, two days after setting out, he referred to 'the mountainous nature of the country' in Devon, and added: 'this day gave me some ideas of the pleasures of travelling and have raised my expectations of future enjoyment to a very high point.'

They sailed to the French port of Morlaix, which gave Faraday a poor impression of France. He thought the Customs very slow and inefficient. They had brought a carriage with them and acquired horses with which they set off for Paris. In Paris, Michael Faraday saw all the tourist sights, and went with Davy on his visits to chemists, laboratories and factories. His *Journal* makes several comparisons between England and France, such as 'French apartments are highly ornamented, English apartments are clean.' After shopping in Paris he wrote: 'It would seem that every tradesman here is a rogue.' His *Journal* reveals Faraday as a keen observer, eager to learn from everything he saw and everything that Davy would explain.

They had hoped to visit a sugar factory early in November, but that did not prove possible. Faraday's first task at the Royal Institution had been to extract sugar from beet in the laboratory, so he was eager to see the process on an industrial scale. This was not just a scientific curiosity. Making sugar from beet was of great economic and political value because it gave Britain an home-grown source of sugar. Most of Britain's sugar came from sugar-cane grown in the West Indies. This made it an expensive commodity, and the supply routes were easily attacked by an enemy in time of war.

The climax of their stay in Paris came later in November when three of the most distinguished French scientists, Ampère, Clément and Desormes, called on Davy to show him a new substance obtained from a certain seaweed. It had been discovered a couple of years previously by Bernard Courtois, who made washing soda from the ashes of burned seaweed. When the new substance was heated, it gave off a purple vapour; this condensed to give shiny dark crystals of the substance. The French chemists soon found that it behaved rather like chlorine. Chemists, however, disagreed about the nature of chlorine. Most believed it was the oxide of an unknown substance, while Sir Humphry Davy, as we have seen, thought it was an element. Davy set to work with the portable chemical set which he always took on his travels.

Faraday was about to witness an important piece of chemical research. It was more than the discovery of a new element: a basic belief held by most chemists was being challenged. They believed that all acids contained oxygen. Indeed, the name 'oxygen' means 'acid maker'. Since chlorine formed an acid (hydrochloric acid) when combined with hydrogen, they believed it must be an oxide. Davy did not accept the oxygen theory of acids, and he believed that chlorine was an element. After several experiments, including an attempt to decompose the new substance by electricity, Davy concluded that what the French chemists had given him was also an element. Still in Paris, he wrote a paper to the Royal Society in London, describing the new substance and proposing the name *Iodine*, from the Greek word for the colour of the vapour.

After Christmas 1813 the party left Paris and continued the journey southwards. During a stay at Montpellier, Faraday casually walked into a fort on a hill above the town. Afterwards he wrote in his *Journal*: 'The stroll round the ramparts was pleasant but I imagine that at times whilst enjoying myself I was transgressing for the sentinels regarded me sharply and more particularly at least I thought so as I stood looking at one corner where from some cause or other the fortifications were injured.' Faraday had no interest in politics, and it probably never occurred to him as strange that he, an Englishman, should wander around a French fort when his country was at war with France.

They travelled on through Italy, reaching Florence in April. Here, Faraday was interested to see the telescope with which Galileo had discovered the satellites of Jupiter. Sir Humphry Davy turned to another scientific problem: the nature of diamond. The Grand Duke of Tuscany had a large burning glass which could be used to burn diamonds by concentrating the rays of the sun. The point of using a burning glass was that it allowed Davy to make the experiment inside a large closed glass vessel, so that he could collect the products of combustion without risking contamination. He confirmed that the only product was pure carbon dioxide, and concluded that diamond was not *chemically* different from graphite and lamp-black (which also gave carbon dioxide when heated), but was a different crystalline form of the same element. They are all carbon.

The party toured Rome and visited Naples, where they climbed Mount Vesuvius and Davy explained the geology of volcanoes to Faraday. The Queen of Naples gave Davy some specimens of colours from the ruined Roman city of Pompeii, which Davy analysed. This was probably the first use of chemistry in archaeology, and it also marked the end of the tour. Davy decided to return home and the party reached London in April 1815, travelling through

6 Sketch from Faraday's Journal of a waterspout seen off the Italian coast.

Switzerland and Germany but not France. The decision to return seems to have been made suddenly, and no reason is given in Faraday's diary. Possibly it was connected with Napoleon's escape from Elba on 26 February, and the subsequent renewed fighting, culminating in the Battle of Waterloo on 18 June.

The tour had been an education for Faraday; he had met some of the leading scientists of Europe including Ampère and the de la Rives. In the following years he maintained a correspondence with Ampère as they developed their ideas about electromagnetism. He also corresponded with the father and son Gaspard and Auguste de la Rive in Geneva, and renewed the friendship with Auguste on his later visits to Europe.

MAN OF SCIENCE

On returning to England, Michael Faraday was employed again by the Royal Institution. He was now Superintendent of the Apparatus and Assistant in the Laboratory and Mineralogical Collection, with a salary of thirty shillings per week and rooms in the Institution building. He was a much more important member of the staff than before his travels. His duties included setting up lecture demonstrations for the Institution staff, especially W T Brande, who had succeeded Davy as Professor of Chemistry. Faraday also helped Brande with his commercial analytical work, and soon became a skilled analytical chemist himself. Faraday's first scientific publications were on analyses - the very first being *Analysis of Native Caustic Lime of Tuscany*, in 1816.

After his return Faraday embarked on a massive task of teaching himself chemistry. Among his books which survive to this day are three volumes of Brande's *Manual of Chemistry* (1819) which Faraday broke apart and rebound with blank pages interleaved with the text. He spent many hours in the Library studying scientific journals and filling the blank pages with detailed notes and references.

Faraday gave a series of lectures to the City Philosophical Society, beginning in January 1816. During this period he made a close and critical study of all the lectures he heard, to master the art of lecturing himself. His *Advice to a Lecturer*, a collection of notes mainly extracted from his correspondence with Abbott, was published in 1960. It is still worthwhile reading for teachers and lecturers. Faraday offered advice on many aspects of the preparation and presentation of lectures, and warned against very long lectures: 'One hour is enough for anyone, and they should not be allowed to exceed that time'.

The Faradays were a deeply religious family. Michael's parents had met and married in the Sandemanian Church at Kirkby Stephen in Westmorland. After moving to London they regularly went to the small Sandemanian chapel in the City, near St Paul's. The Sandemanians were a small, closely-knit evangelical sect which had broken away from the Scottish Presbyterian Church early in the eighteenth century. Their services were simple and their aim was to follow the example of the Christian Church of New Testament times. The members probably seemed rather anti-social since they preferred to find their friends from among fellow members of the sect. They held strong religious beliefs but did not believe in forcing their views on others. They were 'hyper-Calvinist', believing that those who were destined to join them would find their own way in. They thought it wrong to save up money. They had no clergy; the members elected Elders who led the services.

This was the community in which Michael Faraday grew up. He attended the little chapel whenever he could throughout his life, and it was there that he met his future wife, Sarah Barnard, the daughter of a silversmith. They were married in 1821. It was a happy marriage and they were well suited to each other. They had no children of their own, but their nieces were frequent and welcome visitors, and there were times when the Royal Institution building rang with laughter from family parties. Sarah was no intellectual, and she was happy to care for her husband without understanding his work. In her own words, she was 'quite content to be the pillow of his mind'. Faraday, too, did not feel any need to discuss his work with his wife or anyone else. He was a solitary worker; Sergeant Anderson, who had come to help with the glass research, remained with Faraday for the rest of his life, and was the only assistant Faraday ever had.

Faraday kept his religion, his science and his domestic life quite separate. A month after the marriage he formally joined the Church of which his wife was already a member, and in 1840 he was elected an Elder. His sermons, when he was called upon to preach, were constrained by Sandemanian tradition, earnest and dull, quite unlike his lively scientific lectures. But Faraday reading the Bible in Church was different again. A man who often listened to him found it 'one of the richest treats that it has been my good fortune to enjoy'.

Faraday once found himself subject to the strict discipline of his Church; he was deprived of his Eldership and excluded from membership for a time. He had been absent one Sunday without a good enough reason. In fact, he had been invited to dine with Queen Victoria at Windsor! His real 'offence' in the eyes of the church, however, seems to have been that he was not sufficiently penitent when rebuked. Faraday accepted the decision without demur, continuing to worship at the chapel, and in 1860 he was again elected to the Eldership.

Faraday's religion was a very personal matter, rarely spoken of in public. He did mention it in a lecture on education in 1854, but only to say that religious and scientific belief were two different things, and that the reason one applied to science could not be applied to religion. Still, it seems likely that his religious belief in a single Creator encouraged his scientific belief in the 'unity or forces', the idea that magnetism, electricity and other forces have a common origin. For Faraday the Bible was the Word of God to be read and taken at its face value. In the same spirit he sought to read 'the book of nature', finding in the natural world the works of God. Both books should be open to those who tried to read them. On at least two occasions Faraday quoted to a Royal Institution audience a verse from Paul's *Letter to the Romans* (chapter 1, verse 20) which was frequently cited by Sandemanian authors: *For the invisible things of him from the creation of the world are clearly seen, being understood by the things that are made, even his eternal power and Godhead.*

Although firmly convinced that in studying the natural world he was studying the work of God, Faraday was suspicious of any attempt to deduce scientific facts mathematically. Mathematics appears only rarely in Faraday's scientific work, and usually only in such simple forms as showing that two quantities are equal or proportional. His contemporary Charles Babbage spent many years building - or attempting to build - mathematical machines including his 'difference engine' for computing mathematical tables. Faraday is reputed to have said on one occasion that 'the only mathematical operation he had ever performed was turning the handle of the Difference Engine'.

Faraday's way of life was very simple. After about 1834 he rarely went out to dinners and parties. It was not because he disapproved of such things; he preferred to spend his time in scientific research. A letter from his friend, Professor Wheatstone, to a colleague illustrates his approach:

My dear Sir,
I called on Faraday this morning and was informed that this was one of the days on which he denies himself to every body for the purpose of pursuing uninterruptedly his own researches. He will be visible tomorrow, and if you will return me the drawings I will again call upon him.

Yours very truly
C. Wheatstone

Thursday
Oct 4/38

Letter from Charles Wheatstone to W F Cooke

Faraday's income from the Royal Institution was not high compared with the earnings of other scientists, but it was a good income and, by taking on more consulting work, he could have become a rich man. Much of his income went on charity. He often visited the poorer members of his church, helping the needy with his own money.

He was a gentle man, but could be roused to anger. The Government sometimes awarded eminent men 'pensions', annual sums of money to help them carry on work of public interest. In 1835 the Prime Minister, Viscount Melbourne, asked Faraday to call on him because the Government wanted to give him such a pension. In the conversation, Melbourne called the giving of pensions 'humbug'. Faraday promptly left the interview, and wrote to Lord Melbourne declining the offer. However, Faraday's friends would not let the matter end like this. The affair was reported in *The Times*. The result was that the King himself intervened, Melbourne apologised, and Faraday received a pension of £300 per year for the rest of his life.

In 1825 the Managers of the Royal Institution wanted to show their appreciation of Faraday's work. They could not afford to raise his salary, but at Sir Humphry Davy's suggestion they appointed him Director of the Laboratory. In this new position, Faraday began two new activities in the Institution's programme: the first was a weekly evening meeting of members, and the second a series of lectures for children at Christmas. Faraday himself spoke at the first Friday evening meeting, giving a lecture on rubber. The first Christmas lectures were on astronomy, and given by J. Wallis.

The weekly meeting developed into the Friday Evening Discourses, which are still held today. The members and their guests meet in the theatre of the Royal Institution. At 9 p.m. precisely the clock strikes. The speaker enters, and begins his address without any introduction by the chairman. The lecture is often accompanied by slides and experimental demonstrations, and lasts one hour. Faraday himself gave many of the first Friday Evening Discourses, and he also gave several series of the Children's Christmas Lectures. These also continue and have been televised in recent years.

Faraday's lectures were nearly all reporting his own work, but a number of his early Discourses were about the researches of his friend Charles Wheatstone, who became Professor at King's College London and was one of the inventors of the

7 Charles Wheatstone.

19

electric telegraph. Both men liked music, and Wheatstone, who came from a family of musical instrument makers, studied the physics of music and musical instruments. He considered questions such as the way in which sounds can be conducted through solid rods or stretched wires, and how it is that the same musical note sound different when played on different musical instruments.

The physics of sound is an excellent subject for demonstration lectures, but Wheatstone was an intensely shy man and hated to speak in public. On several occasions the Royal Institutions records state that the lecture was 'delivered by Mr. Faraday but supplied by Mr. Wheatstone'.

In 1833 a wealthy member of the Royal Institution, John Fuller, gave a sum of money to endow a professorship. Fuller stipulated that Faraday was to be the first Fullerian Professor of Chemistry. This raised Faraday's income from the Institution to £200 per year, at which it remained until 1853 when it became £300, after he was appointed 'Superintendent of the House and Laboratories'.

8 Faraday lecturing to children at the Royal Institution.

DISCOVERIES IN CHEMISTRY

As his reputation grew, Michael Faraday was in demand as a scientific consultant and expert witness in legal cases. In 1818 a Mr S. Cocks engaged Faraday to help him in a lawsuit about a chemical patent. In 1820 he gave evidence for some insurance companies in a complicated case which arose from a fire in a sugar refinery: was the fire started in the sugar itself, or in a certain oil which was used in the refining process? According to the sugar company, neither the oil nor the vapour from it could catch fire at below 580° Fahrenheit (304°C). Faraday made tests for the insurance companies and found that the vapour could catch fire at the much lower temperature of 382° Fahrenheit (194°C).

The case was decided on other grounds, but the experience had two important results for Faraday. One was that Davy had given evidence for the sugar company, and the incident helped to drive the two men apart. Secondly, while doing his research for the insurance companies, Faraday had become interested in the gases given off when oils are heated. At about the same time, his elder brother Robert had begun to work in the new gas industry in London. The Portable Gas Company sold gas made by heating whale oil, or codfish oil, in a furnace. The gas was stored in high-pressure containers (about thirty times atmospheric pressure). The containers were carried round to the customer's house and used for supplying gas lighting. The Gas Company found that during the bottling process a liquid collected in the apparatus. In 1825 Michael Faraday was asked to analyse this liquid. He found that it was a mixture of substances which evaporated at different temperatures, but most of it was a liquid which boiled at about 186° Fahrenheit (86°C). This, he concluded, must be a single compound. He found by analysis that it was a compound of carbon and hydrogen only, and he found the ratio of the two elements in it. He called the new substance 'bicarburet of hydrogen'. Known today as benzene, it is of basic importance to organic chemistry. It is the simplest substance to have a 'ring' structure. That is, some of the atoms in the molecule are arranged in a ring rather than in a line. Its significance was only realised after 1860, when Kekulé worked out its structure. Faraday deserves the credit for finding a new substance, but he could not have known its significance.

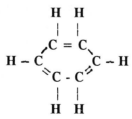

9 The structure of the benzene molecule.

As the son of a blacksmith, Faraday was naturally interested when in 1818 a London cutler, James Stodart, sought help in some researches into steel. Stodart's shop sold 'Surgeon's Instruments, Razors and other Cutlery' made from wootz. This was a steel imported from India. Stodart found it better for his purposes than any steel made in Europe. For more than twenty years he had been trying to make a steel as good or better than wootz, but without success. As a member of the Royal Institution he must have known Faraday, who willingly analysed a specimen of wootz and then tried to manufacture some. But the work failed, and was abandoned for some months.

About this time Faraday was engaged by a South Wales ironmaker to analyse samples and then invited to visit the works. He was always pleased to visit factories and workshops. In July 1819 he set out on a walking tour of Wales, beginning with Mr Guest's iron works at Methyr Tydfil, where he spent several days, and also including Mr Vivian's copper works near Swansea. The diary of his journey includes a description of the South Wales countryside as well as a detailed account of the production of iron and copper. When Faraday came back to work with Stodart on steel, he had a new idea: copper was hardened by alloying it with one of the 'noble' metals, gold or silver. Could steel be hardened in the same way? He built a more powerful furnace, and then made many steel samples by melting iron together with other metals such as platinum, rhodium, silver, nickel and tin. He examined the alloys formed and found that they could indeed produce in the laboratory steels which were better than any steel commercially available in England. The next step was to persuade a manufacturer to adopt the process on a large scale. A firm in Sheffield did try to use the new alloys to make high-quality cutlery, but it was not a success, probably because the alloying metals were so expensive. James Stodart died in 1823, and Faraday lost interest in steel.

In 1823 Faraday obtained liquid chlorine for the first time, using a method suggested by Davy. He heated chlorine hydrate in one arm of a closed tube shaped like an upside-down V. The chlorine gas driven off condensed to liquid in the other arm of the tube, which was kept cold. He then liquefied a number of other gases in the same way.

The work with steels showed that Faraday was well qualified for another research task. In 1824 the Royal Society and the Board of Longitude decided to sponsor research to improve optical glass for navigational instruments. The work was entrusted to John F W Herschel, the astronomer, George Dollond, the optician, and Michael Faraday. Faraday had the practical task of making various kinds of glass. First he studied the processes involved, and analysed various glass samples. Then, in September 1827, a special laboratory with a furnace was provided for the research. An assistant, Sergeant Anderson of the Royal Artillery, was engaged to help.

Glass is made by heating together a number of substances, including sand, potash or soda, and usually lime, magnesia or lead oxide. Faraday was trying to make a very heavy glass, with as much lead as possible. It was thought that this would have the best optical properties. The work was beset with difficulties. Often, when the samples were examined after cooling, he found the glass was cracked or contained bubbles or bands of colour where the ingredients had not mixed properly. If he stirred the molten glass in the furnace the pot containing it usually broke. He tried using a platinum

10 Royal Institution laboratory in Faraday's time, from a water colour by Harriet Moore.

dish to hold the mixture in the furnace, but whenever a drop of molten glass splashed onto the iron supports the lead oxide in the glass reacted with the iron, leaving pure lead metal. Unfortunately, lead reacts with platinum to form an alloy which melted in the furnace. So whenever any of the lead touched the dish it reacted - and left a hole in the dish. Several times Faraday put in his notebook that 'bottom of the platina vessel disappeared... and the experiment was suddenly put an end to.'

This was but one of many difficulties Faraday had to face, explain and overcome. Finally, in April 1829, he produced a piece of glass he could describe as 'good', and which Dollond could make into a lens. He continued to work on glass sporadically for another couple of years, but by 1831 circumstances had changed. The finances of the Royal Institution had improved, and the income from the steel and glass research projects was no longer so important.

Faraday wanted to devote his whole time to another topic: electricity.

CHEMISTRY

The industrial revolution began in the eighteenth century with the introduction of the steam engine. This made mechanical power available for pumping water out of mines and for driving factory machinery. When Faraday was born the chemical industry was beginning to develop. A major chemical process was the manufacture of soap. In 1785 some 15,000 tons were produced annually in Britain. By 1830 production had risen to over 50,000 tons.

Soap is made by heating together alkalis and fat. The fats may be almost any animal or vegetable fats; the alkalis, in the eighteenth century, were obtained from the ashes of various plants, mainly certain seaweeds. Alkalis were also used in the textile industry and in glass manufacture. Textiles in particular were an expanding industry, and consequently there was a potential shortage of alkali. This was felt more acutely in France than in Britain, and the French Académie des Sciences offered a substantial prize for a new source of alkali.

In 1789 Nicolas LeBlanc devised a process which became the world's principle source of alkali for over a century. It consisted of heating together sodium sulphate, chalk (calcium carbonate) and coal (largely carbon). The sodium sulphate was obtained by reacting sulphuric acid (made by burning sulphur) with common salt.

When Faraday and Sir Humphry Davy visited France in 1813 they were visiting a country with an advanced chemical industry, and doubtless studied all they could. He had been invited, with Napoleon's approval, to study the chemistry of some volcanic rocks. No new discoveries came of that, though while in France Davy examined a newly discovered substance, iodine, which French chemists had extracted from seaweed. He showed that it was a new element, and similar in its properties to chlorine.

The illustration shows the Chemical Laboratory at the Royal Institution as it was in the early nineteenth century. This is where Davy, and then Faraday, did much of their chemical work.

Davy's reputation as a chemist was based on two particular areas of research. He had shown that chlorine was an element, and so brought into question an established chemical theory. Chlorine reacts with hydrogen to form hydrochloric acid, and that was well known. The French chemist Antoine Lavoisier had suggested that all acids contain oxygen (the name *oxy-gen* is Greek and means 'acid maker'.) If that were true then chlorine must be a compound of oxygen and an unknown element, which was called 'murium'. The substances now called 'chlorides' were then called 'muriates'.

Davy had also used electrolysis to obtain the elements sodium, potassium, calcium, strontium and barium for the first time.

FIRST DISCOVERIES IN ELECTRICITY AND MAGNETISM

Faraday's first electrical discovery was made in 1821. In the previous October the Danish scientist, Hans Christian Oersted, had made an important discovery. He found that an electric current flowing through a wire produced a magnetic effect. If the wire were held above a compass needle, the needle would turn at right angles to the wire when the current flowed. If the wire was held under the compass, but with the current still flowing in the same direction, then the needle turned the other way.

11 Hans Christian Oersted.

Oersted's discovery was published in Latin, still a widely understood language at the time, under the title *Experimenta circa effectum conflictus electrici in acum magneticum.* It created great interest for two reasons. The first was that before Oersted's discovery many people, including Faraday, believed that there must be some link between electricity and magnetism. Now it was proved. Secondly, the relationship was a strange one, which is probably why it had not been found sooner. The force between two magnets tends either to bring them together or to push them apart. The force between electrically charged objects behaves in a similar way, and the force of gravity always tends to bring objects together. These are all called 'central forces' because they act between one centre and another. But the current in Oersted's wire did not pull the compass needle towards the wire, nor did it push it away. Instead the current produced a magnetic force which seemed to act in a circle around the wire. It caused a sensation, and every scientist who read Oersted's paper tried the experiment for himself. The phenomenon was named 'electromagnetism'.

Two main ideas were suggested to explain electromagnetism. Some scientists thought that the wire carrying an electric current must itself become a magnet, and that electromagnetism was the interaction of two magnets - the

26

compass needle and the wire. The Austrian J J Prechtl explained it in this way by suggesting that wire carrying an electric current became magnetised with the left-hand side of the wire as one magnetic pole, and the right-hand side as the other. That would explain the deflection when the needle was above or below the wire, and it could be explained in terms of central forces, not circular ones.

But it left open the question why the wire became magnetised in that particular way. The Frenchman A-M Ampère (whose name was later adopted for the 'ampère' or 'amp', the unit of electric current) took the other view. He saw everything in terms of electric currents. He said that every permanent magnet contained circulating electric currents, and he showed that there was a force between two parallel wires carrying a current.

In England W H Wollaston also tried to explain electromagnetism by the existence of circulating currents. But he said that it was the current in the wire which 'circulated' and took a helical path along the wire. Wollaston thought that, because of the circulating path of the current, a wire would tend to rotate on its own axis when a magnet was brought near. In April 1821 he and Davy tried to make a wire rotate in that way, but failed.

Faraday took little part in these speculations at that time, partly because he was busy making steel alloys for James Stodart (as well as courting Sarah Barnard), and partly because he was no mathematician and the theories being propounded were mostly very mathematical and had little experimental basis. Later Faraday wrote to Ampère, saying, 'Your theory ... so soon becomes mathematical that it quickly gets beyond my reach.'

12 André-Marie Ampère.

In the summer of 1821 Faraday's friend Phillips, editor of the scientific journal, *The Annals of Philosophy*, invited him to write an historical account of electromagnetism. With his usual thoroughness, Faraday repeated all the important experiments of the other scientists while writing his account. As he studied the subject, he became convinced that it ought to be possible to produce continuous circular movement by making use of the circular magnetic force

Plate IV. *Vol.* 2. *Exp. Researches.*

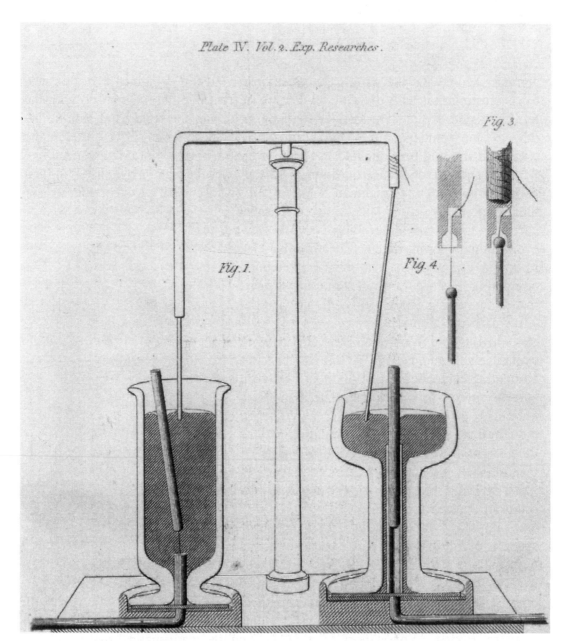

13 Faraday's demonstration of electromagnetic rotation, from his *Experimental Researches in Electricity.*

around a wire. In September 1821 he found how to do it. In fact, he built two devices, which have been called the first electric motors, to show 'electromagnetic rotation'.

In the first, he fixed a bar magnet vertically in a basin with a blob of wax. The basin was then nearly filled with mercury. A wire with a cork on its end was loosely fixed to a point above the basin, and a battery connected between the wire and another wire which dipped into the edge of the basin. 'Very satisfactory', wrote Faraday in his notebook, after seeing the wire move in circles around the magnet. In the second arrangement, the magnet was fixed at the bottom, so that the upper end was free to move. The wire from above dipped into the middle of the mercury. This way, the upper end of the magnet moved in circles around the fixed wire.

Faraday then had a special demonstration apparatus made which combined the rotating wire arrangement and the rotating magnet one. This apparatus was copied and the experiments were repeated all over Europe. But Faraday's haste in announcing a discovery which brought him fame also created a most unpleasant situation. It was well known that Wollaston had tried to make a wire revolve by electromagnetism; and at a quick glance Faraday's experiment was almost the same as Wollaston's. Faraday did not mention Wollaston's experiment when he published his own discovery, and many people thought at first that he had copied Wollaston's experiment without giving him credit. In fact, Faraday had been unable to contact Wollaston quickly, and did not like to quote his work without permission. Faraday's arrangement was really quite distinct from Wollaston's, but the incident caused much ill feeling just when Faraday was being proposed for Fellowship of the Royal Society. He was elected, but the decision was not unanimous. Sadly, it seems to have been Sir Humphry Davy who led the opposition to him.

14 A Cruickshank battery - the kind of battery used by Faraday for many of his electrical experiments.

ELECTRIC MOTORS

Faraday's demonstration of continuous movement produced by electricity and magnetism has been called the first 'electric motor'. That is perhaps an exaggeration, but the experiment demonstrated the possibility. A better candidate for the title may be the device Peter Barlow (1776-1862) described in a letter to Faraday. Barlow's

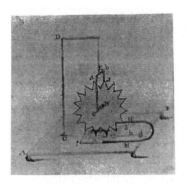

sketch, reproduced here, shows a star-shaped wheel mounted between the poles of a horse-shoe magnet and dipping into mercury. When a current was passed between the axis of the wheel and the mercury then the wheel rotated.

Several people studied electromagnets (a coil of wire wound on an iron core and carrying an electric current) and they attempted to make machines which produced motion by switching electromagnets on and off and attracting pieces of iron. One such machine was described by Joseph Henry (1797-1878) who wrote in 1831: 'I have lately succeeded in producing motion in a little machine by a power which, I believe, has never before been applied in mechanics - by magnetic attraction and repulsion.'

Faraday did not often take much interest in the practical applications of electricity, but the idea of 'electromagnetic engines' seems to have appealed to him. In 1832 he wrote to the Russian Professor M. H. Jacobi of St. Petersburg: 'To think only of putting an electromagnetic machine into the *Great Western* or the *British Queen* and sending them across the Atlantic by it or even to the East Indies! What a glorious thing it would be.'

Jacobi had a grant from the Czar for research into electric power, which must surely be the first government grant anywhere for electrical research.

William Sturgeon (1783-1850) made a motor in 1832 which did useful work - it turned a roasting spit. Sturgeon invented the commutator, which enabled electrical connections to be made through metal 'brushes' to the moving part.

All these machines depended on batteries for their electricity, so the power they produced was very expensive compared with steam power. Despite much ingenuity by many people there could be no future for electric motors until electricity itself was available at a reasonable price. When electric generators became readily available in the 1870s people soon found that if two direct current generators were connected together one machine could act as a motor. The first practical motors were therefore similar to the generators. An electric railway was demonstrated in Berlin in 1879; during the 1880s electric trains were developed in Germany, Britain and the USA.

The first practical alternating current motors were developed by Nicola Tesla (1856-1943) who was born in what is now Yugoslavia, but emigrated to the USA. His motors had fixed coils which were connected to the alternating current supply and so arranged that they created a rotating magnetic field. The moving part of the motor was drawn round by the rotating field, either at the same speed (*synchronous* motors), or a little slower (*induction* motors). Most of the electric power in factories comes from these types of motor.

Induction and synchronous motors are more robust than direct current motors, but their speed cannot easily be varied. The speed of direct current motors is easily controlled, and so they have been preferred for some purposes such as electric trains.

With the availability in recent years of 'power semiconductors' capable of switching quite heavy currents there have been further developments in motors. 'Switched reluctance machines', as they are called, combine the robustness of AC machines with the easy control of DC ones. There are no commutators or brushes to wear out: the necessary switching of current in the coils is carried out entirely by solid-state electronics.

FURTHER DISCOVERIES IN ELECTRICITY AND MAGNETISM

If an electric current could produce magnetic effects, could electricity be produced from magnetism? This was the question to which Faraday returned from time to time during the 1820s, but without success. He was inclined to accept Ampère's theory that magnetic effects were caused by electric currents, and he thought that if two wires were placed side by side and a current made to flow in one wire then some electric effect should be produced in the other.

In 1825 Faraday took two pieces of wire about 1.5 metres long, tied them together with just a single thickness of paper between them, and connected one to a battery. A galvanometer was connected to the other wire, but it showed nothing. Faraday returned to his research on glass.

The Frenchman, Dominique François Jean Arago (1786-1853), made an important discovery in 1824; he found that there was a force between a magnet and a *moving* copper plate. Arago had acquired a new compass and he noticed that it was heavily damped: in other words, instead of oscillating violently and gradually settling down, the needle came to rest quite quickly in its final position. He investigated and found that this was because the compass had a copper base. If a fixed copper base tended to discourage movement of the needle, what would a moving one do? Arago pivoted a compass needle over a copper disc and made the disc go round. He found that the compass needle also went round, in the same direction as the disc. Subsequently it was found that if a magnet is rotated close to an electrically conducting disc, then the disc tends to follow the magnet, and also that the effect is lessened if radial slits are cut in the plate.

These discoveries proved important when, in 1831, Faraday again turned from chemistry to electricity. They suggested that the effect was due to electricity being produced in some way in the disc.

The statues of Faraday (there is one in the Royal Institution and one on the Victoria Embankment near Waterloo Bridge) show him holding a piece of apparatus in his left hand. This is his 'induction ring', with which he made the greatest of his discoveries on 29 August 1831. The discovery was electromagnetic induction: the induction (or generation) of electricity in a wire by means of the electromagnetic effect of a current in another wire. The section in Faraday's notebook is headed 'Expts on the production of Electricity from Magnetism &c'. It describes the first of a series of brilliant discoveries made during the autumn of 1831, which form the basis of modern electrical technology. The induction ring was the first electric transformer. (A later discovery in the series was the first generator).

The induction ring is a simple device. Faraday wound two coils of wire on a ring of soft iron about twenty millimetres thick and 150 mm in diameter. As the wire was bare metal, he wound a piece of calico under each layer of wire and a piece of fine string between the turns. In that way each part of the wire was insulated both from the iron ring and from the adjacent turns. Each coil was wound in several parts, with both ends of each part brought out. This allowed him to use either the whole coil or just a part of it. He connected one coil (which he called 'B') to a piece of wire which passed over a compass about one metre away from the ring. After describing the ring and windings, Faraday wrote: 'connected the ends of one of the pieces on a side with battery. Immediately a sensible effect on needle. It oscillated and settled at last in original position. On *breaking* connection of A side with Battery again a disturbance of the needle.'

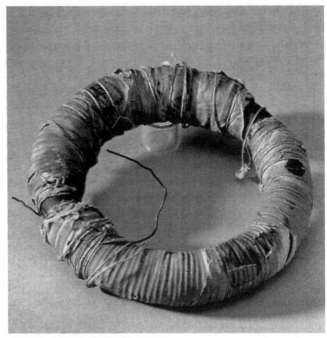

15 Faraday's induction ring.

There was an effect in coil B when a current began to flow in coil A. This was 'electromagnetic induction', the induction of electricity by means of electromagnetism. With more tests, he found that iron did not have to be used. He could show the effect with two coils wound on a cardboard tube, though it was much greater when the iron core was there.

When the experiment was made without the iron core, it was very like the 1825 experiment. Faraday had tied together two pieces of wire, connected the first one to a battery and looked for an indication on a galvanometer connected to the second. Why did he fail to find the effect in 1825? His apparatus had probably been improved by 1831, but his understanding had also changed. In

1825 he expected the mere presence of a current in the first wire to produce an effect in the second. By 1831 he expected a new factor to be involved. This new factor was a movement or a change in something. He expected an effect in the second coil at the moment he completed the circuit of the first coil and battery. At that moment the current in the first coil changed, from nothing to something and, because he was looking for an effect then, he found it. The compass needle swung to one side, oscillated to and fro, and finally settled in its original position. When the circuit of the first coil was broken, so that the current changed back to nothing, there was a similar effect; but the compass needle moved first in the opposite direction.

The discovery of electromagnetic induction was important for Faraday. He had been searching for some such effect on and off for ten years, and it helped his theoretical understanding of electricity and magnetism. The discovery is important to us for another reason. The induction ring was the first electric transformer and our modern electrical world depends on vast numbers of transformers.

Although Faraday's discovery of electromagnetic induction was noted under the heading 'Expts on the production of Electricity from Magnetism &c.' he had not yet produced electricity from magnetism. This he sought to do in the following weeks.

He gathered together a variety of coils of wire, magnets and pieces of iron. Success came on 2 September 1831, when he was experimenting with two bar magnets and a cylindrical coil wound on an iron bar. The two magnets and the iron bar were arranged in a triangular manner to form a complete 'magnetic circuit', and the coil was connected to a galvanometer. When the magnetic circuit was broken, by removing the iron bar, the galvanometer showed a brief electric current. On putting the iron bar back a brief current flowed the opposite way. This was undoubtedly magnetism being converted into electricity. Faraday called it magneto-electric induction (the induction of electricity by means of a magnet) to distinguish it from his earlier discovery of electromagnetic induction.

In October of the same year Faraday found another way of arranging his coils and magnets to produce magneto-electric induction. Using a coil wound on a hollow paper cylinder he found that electricity was induced in the coil if a bar magnet was either thrust quickly into the coil, or pulled quickly out.

When this fact became known several scientists, though apparently not Faraday, made hand-operated generators in which either a magnet was moved to and fro inside a fixed coil, or a coil was moved to and fro in front of a permanent magnet. (The modern electric generator uses *rotary* motion between the magnet and the coil, rather than a to-and-fro motion in a straight line.) The first such generator was made in Paris by a young French instrument maker, Hippolyte Pixii. All the generators in power stations today have developed from the machine Pixii made after reading of Faraday's discoveries.

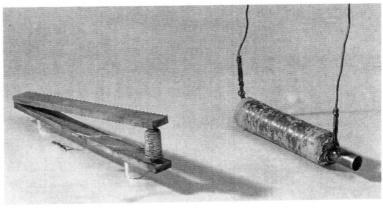

16 Coils and magnets used by Faraday.

Faraday did make one generator himself, but it was quite different from Pixii's. Pixii's machine produced alternating current as the coils passed from the north pole of the magnet to the south pole and then back to the north pole again. Faraday wanted a machine that would produce a steady direct current, like a battery. For that he needed to make a conductor move *continuously in the same direction* past the poles of a magnet. That may sound impossible, but it can be done if the conductor is part of a rotating copper disc. He arranged the disc to spin between the poles of a large permanent magnet and made two sliding connections with pieces of springy metal. One connection was on the axis, and the other on the edge of the disc near the magnet. While the disc was moving, electricity was induced in the part of the disc between the sliding contacts. In this way a continuous output was obtained. Faraday's 'disc generator' is of little practical use, but it showed how much he had learned about electricity and magnetism. It also enabled him to explain Arago's discovery that a copper plate would damp down the oscillations of a compass. The movement of the magnetic needle generated electric currents in the disc, and these in turn produced a magnetic field which acted on the compass to oppose its movement.

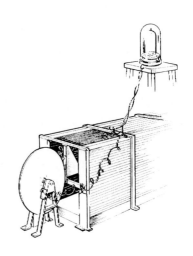

17 Faraday's disc generator.

TRANSFORMERS AND GENERATORS

The induction ring experiment of 1831 showed that a current in one wire could produce an electrical effect in another. The two wires were both coiled on a soft iron ring, and Faraday found that a current was induced in the second wire when the current in the first was either made or broken. Nothing happened when the current in the first was steady.

The first development of this was the Ruhmkorff coil, or induction coil. This has a device which rapidly makes and breaks the circuit in one coil (the 'primary') and so induces a high voltage in the other (the 'secondary'). Faraday used an induction coil when pursuing his research on electrical discharges in gases.

Transformers are an essential component of the electricity supply system. They were first used in electricity supply by Gaulard and Gibbs in 1883, in a series circuit, and then used as they are today by Ferranti.

The generators in power stations work most efficiently if they are designed to generate electricity at a much higher voltage than is safe for domestic use. Sending electrical energy over many miles needs even higher voltages, to be done economically. So the voltage has to be changed several times between the generator and the customer. All these changes of voltage are made by transformers, which are basically iron cores with two coils of wire wound on them.

If coil A of Faraday's induction ring were linked to the ordinary electricity supply, there would be a current in it which was always changing and so electricity would constantly be induced in coil B. If the coils A and B have the same number of turns, the voltage in the circuit of coil B will be about the same as coil A. If B has more or less turns than A, then the voltage in its circuit will be more, or less, in proportion to the number of turns.

Also in 1831 Faraday showed that moving a permanent magnet near a wire - preferably a coil - produced a current in the wire. His most practical variant was the disc generator, in which the radius of a disc acts as a moving conductor passing between the poles of an horseshoe magnet.

The basic idea was quickly taken up by Hippolyte Pixii in Paris, and then by numerous scientific instrument makers.

Magnetos, short for magneto-electric generators, were used in telegraphy and in electroplating from about 1840.

Subsequent developments were the idea of using electromagnets in place of permanent magnets (an idea expressed in 1840 but implemented later), and the self-excited generator in 1866. Really practical machines were developed in the 1870s by Gramme and others. The scientific understanding of the machine comes with Hopkinson in the mid 1880s.

The illustration below shows a generator made by Gramme in the early 1880s which is similar to many machines of the period.

DISCOVERIES IN ELECTROCHEMISTRY

Water breaks down into hydrogen and oxygen when an electric current passes through it. This fact was demonstrated in 1800 only a few months after the Italian scientist, Alessandro Volta, made his 'pile'. Volta's pile was the first electric battery, the first source of a continous electric current. It consisted of a pile of pairs of plates or discs of two different metals (Volta preferred silver and zinc). These were interleaved with pieces of spongy material, such as cloth or cardboard, soaked in salt water. Among the many scientists who quickly made their own pile were two Englishmen, William Nicholson and Anthony Carlisle. Nicholson was a chemist and also editor of a scientific journal; Carlisle was a surgeon. Their pile consisted of seventeen silver coins and the same number of discs of copper and pieces of cloth soaked in salt water. When wires connected to the two ends of the pile were dipped in a vessel of water, they found that gas was given off at each wire. On collecting the gases they found that it was hydrogen given off at the negative wire and oxygen at the positive one. The volume of the hydrogen was twice the volume of the oxygen, and they correctly deduced that they had decomposed some of the water into its elements. This process became known as *electrolysis*, which means loosening by electricity.

It was soon found that a variety of substances could be decomposed if they were first dissolved in water, and an electric current then passed through the solution. If copper sulphate was used, it was found that pure copper metal was deposited on the positive wire. This led to the new industry of electroplating, in which a coating of a more expensive metal such as silver is deposited on cutlery or other objects made of a cheaper metal, and connected to the positive wire of an electrochemical cell. In his early years at the Royal Institution, Humphry Davy made a study of electrochemistry and obtained several previously unknown elements, including sodium and potassium in 1807, and magnesium, calcium and barium in 1808.

Faraday noticed that water will conduct electricity, but ice will not. He made a systematic study of substances which could be melted to find out how well they conducted in both the solid and liquid states. He found that metals always conduct electricity and fatty substances never do. Almost everything else conducted electricity when in its liquid form, but not when solid. The last group of substances were all compounds; when an electric current was passed through the substance in its melted state, chemical decomposition took place.

All Faraday's work so far had been qualitative: he had been observing the nature of various effects but not measuring quantities. He now set out to measure the quantity of chemical effect produced by a certain amount of electricity. If the chemical product was a gas, he measured its volume; if it was a solid, he weighed it. He found that the chemical effect was always in proportion to how much electricity flowed, whatever the size or shape of the apparatus. In his own words: 'chemical action or decomposing power is exactly proportional to the quantity of electricity which passes.' This is the *First Law of Electrolysis*. Every substance which can be discharged in an electrochemical process (such as hydrogen or oxygen in the electrolysis of water, or copper in copper plating) has an *electrochemical equivalent*. This is the weight of substance given off when a standard quantity of electricity passes through the electrochemical cell.

Faraday made an instrument for measuring quantity of electricity, based on the first law. He called it the 'volta electrometer' because it measured electricity from a Volta's pile. The name was soon shortened to 'voltameter'. In its simplest form, it was a glass tube in which two platinum wires were fixed. The tube was filled with water containing a little acid to increase its electrical conductivity. To measure the quantity of electricity flowing in a circuit, the volta electrometer was included in the circuit. As the current flowed, the water was electrolysed, yielding oxygen and hydrogen gases; the volume of the gas could be read on a scale on the side of the tube.

The volume of gas was directly proportional to the quantity of electricity which had

18 A voltameter used by Faraday.

passed. So, if a second electrochemical cell was put in the circuit, Faraday could measure with the volta electrometer how much electricity passed through the second cell. In this way he measured the electrochemical equivalent of a great many substances. He established the *Second Law of Electrolysis*, which says that the electrochemical equivalent of a substance is proportional to its ordinary chemical equivalent. (The chemical equivalent of a substance is the number of grams of it which combines with eight grams of oxygen).

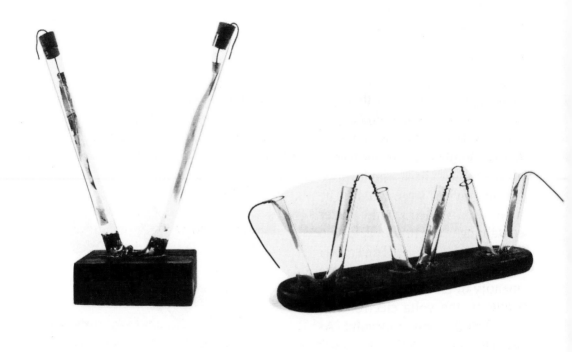

19 **Apparatus used by Faraday in his electrochemical experiments.**

When advances are made in any branch of science, new technical words and phrases often have to be invented. As Faraday went deeper into electro-chemical action, he found he needed a number of new words, partly because he was describing new things but partly also because existing words were often associated in people's minds with old theories and ideas which Faraday himself did not accept. At this time most scientists still thought of electricity as an 'imponderable fluid'. Some looked on electrochemical reactions as processes in which the 'electric fluid' formed chemical compounds with other substances. Faraday himself saw electricity as a force which acted on substances, rather than as a substance itself. To avoid any misunderstandings Faraday decided to introduce a series of new words when publishing his results.

Faraday discussed the choice of words with a number of language experts, including the Revd William Whewell (1794-1866), the Master of Trinity College Cambridge, who had helped Charles Lyell devise words for his geological nomenclature three years earlier. Faraday was himself interested in words. Later, when the word *scientist* came into the English language in 1840, he wrote to Whewell, saying he thought it a good word and asking Whewell to invent something better than *physicist* which, said Faraday, was 'so awkward that I think I shall never be able to use it'. After some correspondence, in which Whewell rejected several of Faraday's first suggestions, they agreed on a series of terms which remain in use today. These new words were used in January 1834 when Faraday published a paper setting out his discoveries in electrochemistry.

The liquid he called the *electrolyte*. The connections where the electric current entered and left the liquid he called *electrodes*. The *anode* was the electrode connected to the positive side of the battery, and the other was the *cathode*. The electrolyte, or the part of it which was decomposed, divided into two *ions*; the ions which went to the anode were called *anions* and the others *cations*.

When water is decomposed the water itself is the electrolyte; the anion is oxygen and the cation is hydrogen. In electroplating, the object being plated forms the cathode and the cation is the metal being deposited.

ELECTROCHEMISTRY

Faraday's work established the principles of electrochemistry, and one application, electroplating, was developed commercially during the 1840s. Sometimes the electricity was supplied by magnetos, and in other cases batteries were used.

Although electroplating is still of commercial importance, the main industrial application of electrochemistry today is the production of some materials by electrolysis. Most chlorine, a major raw material in the chemical industry, is produced by the electrolysis of brine (common salt dissolved in water). Aluminium and copper are also produced by electrolysis.

The illustration shows a typical cell for the electrolysis of brine. The anodes are graphite, the cathodes steel, and the body of the cell is concrete. Chlorine gas is drawn off through pipes at the top. The other product of the electrolysis is sodium which, in this cell, reacts with the water to form sodium hydroxide (caustic soda) and is drawn off through a diaphragm whose function is to keep the products apart. An alternative design of cell uses a mercury cathode. The sodium dissolves in the mercury, which flows continuously through the cell and the sodium is extracted afterwards.

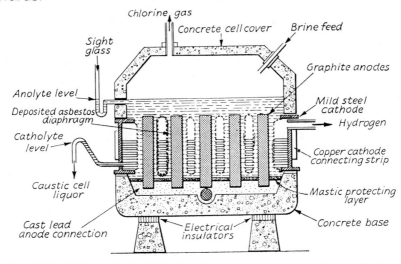

THE NATURE OF ELECTRICITY
AND MAGNETISM

In August 1832, Faraday began another series of electrical researches. This time he was not trying to find new effects, but to show that all kinds of electricity were in fact the same thing. Although he thought that the electricity he had produced from a magnet by induction was the same as volta-electricity (electricity from a battery), and that both were the same as static electricity, he had not actually proved it. Having made the disc generator, which produced a continuous current of magneto-electricity, it was easy to show that magneto-electricity and volta-electricity produced the same effects.

The current from both sources would heat a fine wire, produce magnetism, and cause chemical decomposition when passed through certain liquids, including water. It was much harder to show that static electricity was the same. Magneto-electricity and volta-electricity were characterised by their heating, magnetic and chemical effects. But static electricity involved the attraction and repulsion of charged bodies and the production of sparks. Could these two 'electricities' really be the same?

Faraday realised that the apparent difference between static electricity produced by his frictional machine and electricity from batteries and magneto devices, was that the static electricity was at a much higher 'tension' or voltage. He proved that it could produce magnetic effects by connecting his frictional machine to a sensitive galvanometer by a wet thread. When the machine was turned the galvanometer needle moved.

The heating effect was measurable using a device made by his friend William Snow Harris. The 'electrometer', as it was called, consisted of a glass bulb containing air which was heated by the current in a thin wire which passed through the bulb. A U shaped tube connected to the bulb contained water, and when the air was heated it expanded and the water moved.

For his first demonstration of chemical effects, his apparatus consisted of two silver wires dipped into a solution of copper sulphate. He knew that if an electric current from a battery were passed from one wire to the other through the solution, then one wire would become plated with copper. He fixed one silver wire to his frictional machine and the other to earth. After about a hundred turns of the machine he found a deposit of copper on one of the wires. So static electricity could indeed produce chemical effects.

It had been known for years that volta-electricity could produce sparks;

Humphry Davy had shown that before Faraday went to the Royal Institution. Faraday himself had shown that his magneto-electricity could produce a small spark, though the experiment proved difficult because the spark was so feeble.

The force between bodies charged with static electricity is best seen with an electroscope. In this device two pieces of gold leaf are suspended on a piece of metal fixed in the top of a glass jar. When the charge from a frictional electric machine is passed to the metal, the gold leaves become charged with the same polarity, and so repel each other. Faraday showed that the current from a battery could also charge the electroscope. In other words, static electricity and voltaic and magneto-electricity all produced similar effects. There was only one type of electricity, not two or three.

There were two other sources of 'electricities' which Faraday studied in an effort to show that they also were the same. One was 'thermo-electricity' and the other 'animal electricity'. Despite many trials, he was unable to prove that the shock given by various electric fishes, such as the torpedo,

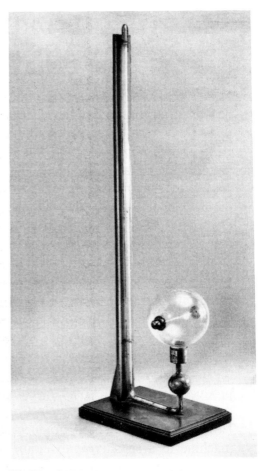

20 Harris Electrometer used by Faraday.

was caused by the same kind of electricity. But he was convinced that it must be so. Some of these trials were made with the help of his friend Professor Wheatstone. The entries in Faraday's diary are brief, and we cannot tell how he set about getting electricity from the fish. Once he wrote, 'Tried Mr Wheatstone's apparatus. It did not do.' Alas, Faraday did not say what 'it' was or what it did not do - but it is comforting for modern students to know that even Faraday's experiments sometimes failed completely!

Faraday had more success with thermo-electricity. If two different metals are joined into a circuit, with one junction kept cold and the other heated, current will flow. But the voltage is so small that it is very hard to produce a spark.

Faraday did not see a 'thermo-electric spark' until 1837, when he met with Wheatstone and the American Professors Henry and Bache in Wheatstone's laboratory at King's College London. It was Professor Henry's apparatus which finally produced the spark, and when he saw it Faraday jumped up with excitement, shouting 'Hurrah for the Yankee experiment!'

Having demonstrated that the various kinds of electricity produced similar effects he set out to relate them numerically. He measured how much electricity came from a battery by timing the period for which it was connected; he said that the quantity of electricity which came from a frictional electric machine depended on the number of turns of the handle. He noted, for example, that the electric current from his battery during eight beats of his watch produced the same magnetic and chemical effects as the electricity from his frictional machine when the handle was turned round thirty times.

In a dramatic experiment in 1835 he had a large wooden cage covered with conducting material built in the middle of the lecture theatre. The cage was insulated from the floor and connected to a frictional electric machine. Faraday's assistant then charged up the cage so that sparks flew from it. Meanwhile Faraday, sitting inside the cage, found that even with his most delicate apparatus he could detect no electric effects. Whatever it was that happened when a body was charged, it took place in the space between the surface of the body and its surroundings.

21 Apparatus for studying the specific inductive capacity of various materials.

He decided to examine the space, and to do this had two sets of apparatus made consisting of two concentric spheres. The outer sphere could be opened so that the insulating material in the space could be changed. If the two sets of apparatus were connected and charged by a frictional electric machine, the 'tension' or voltage between the inner and outer spheres would be the same. If the two devices were then disconnected and connected separately to a gold-leaf electroscope, each would produce the same deflection of the leaves. But when Faraday made the experiment again with different materials in the two spaces, he found that the two devices produced different deflections of the leaves. So the quantity of electric charge on the two devices somehow depended upon the insulating substance. The relationship between the charge and the tension he called the *specific inductive capacity* of the substance. This relationship is now known as the *dielectric constant*.

These experiments showed that something happened in an insulating material which was subjected to electric forces. Faraday made a search for some other evidence of that something. He found two effects which he could not explain, but which helped the advance of physical science and are known by his name. They are the *Faraday effect* and *Faraday's dark space*.

Faraday believed that there must be some basic connection between all the forces of nature. It had been shown that there was a close connection between electricity and magnetism, and by 1845 he was convinced that they must be connected in some way with light. In that year, he found the 'Faraday effect'. This occurs when polarised light passes through a suitable transparent material in the presence of a magnetic field. Polarised light is light in which the vibrations are all (or mostly) in the same plane, and the transparent material in which he found the effect was a piece of heavy glass he had made for the Royal Society about twenty years earlier. Faraday found that when no magnet was present the light passed through the glass unchanged. But when a powerful magnet was brought near the glass, the plane of polarisation was turned.

This experiment suggested to Faraday that a powerful magnet might have some effect on the glass, even though glass is not magnetic. He suspended a piece of glass very delicately between the poles of a large horse-shoe electromagnet, and found that the glass tended to turn **across** the magnetic lines of force (a piece of magnetic material would have tended to turn so as to lie **along** the magnetic lines of force). He called the new phenomenon *diamagnetism*. After testing many substances he found that most things are diamagnetic, though a few non-magnetic substances tend to set themselves along the lines of force. These are called *paramagnetic*.

The 'dark space' was found when he examined electric discharges in air. The apparatus he used for this, which he called the 'electric egg', consisted of an egg-shaped glass bulb with two metal balls mounted inside. With an air pump the pressure inside could be reduced to a very small value, and the metal balls were connected to a source of electricity. Faraday found that, if the voltage was high enough, there was a luminous discharge between the two balls. However, under certain conditions, the discharge was not continuous from one ball to the other, but was broken by a dark region near the cathode (the ball connected to the negative side of the source). He could not explain the effect, but he recorded carefully what he saw and described it in his 1857 Christmas Lectures.

Faraday tried to find a link between gravity and electricity by searching for electrical effects in falling bodies. His last experiment, in 1862, was

22 Faraday's 'electric egg'.

to look for a change in the wavelength of light when passed through a strong magnetic field. He did not find any change: his ideas were right but his apparatus was not sensitive enough. This effect is now known as the Zeeman effect after the Dutch physicist Pieter Zeeman who found it in 1896.

Although he made no more fundamental scientific discoveries his ideas prompted lines of thought in other researchers.

Most scientists tried to explain electrical and magnetic phenomena by considering the points at which the forces appeared to act, such as an electrically charged body or the poles of a magnet. Faraday directed attention to the space in between. What happened *in the space* was more significant than the nature of the points to or from which the force was directed. People had thought of natural forces as acting in a straight line between two bodies. Those forces might be the gravitational attraction between the sun and the earth, or the attraction between a magnet and a piece of iron. In either case the force acted along a straight line and the action was instantaneous.

That basic concept of forces always acting along straight lines was shattered by Oersted's experiment. The compass needle was deflected by a magnetic field produced by a current in a wire, and that magnetic field went round the wire in a circle. Using iron filings to illustrate the lines of magnetic force around a magnet also showed that the forces could act in curved paths. (Faraday first used the terms *lines of magnetic force* and *magnetic curves* in 1831). Having observed that the force was not straight, he also wondered whether it was instantaneous. The idea that forces might take time to act was quite radical and Faraday did not feel sufficiently confident to express the idea publicly. On 12 March 1832 he wrote a sealed note which was deposited in the Royal Society's safe. The note was never opened in Faraday's lifetime, but he spoke about his speculations in 1846. The occasion was a Friday Evening Discourse at the Royal Institution when Faraday was speaking first on Wheatstone's Chronoscope. Having described the instrument, which was designed for measuring short intervals of time such as the time of flight of a projectile, he continued with 'thoughts on ray vibrations'. Subsequently he set down his ideas in a letter to the *Philosophical Magazine*.

Faraday remarked that he 'had to appear suddenly and occupy the place of another'. That comment led to a story, now Royal Institution legend, that Wheatstone had been due to deliver the lecture but, being a very shy man, he had refused at the last minute. In fact the speaker originally booked was James Napier, but he had withdrawn at least a week earlier and Faraday had a week in which to prepare.

Certain of the results of the investigations which are embodied in the two papers entitled <u>Experimental researches in Electricity</u>, lately read to the Royal Society, and the views arising therefrom, in connexion with other views and experiments, lead me to believe that magnetic action is progressive, and requires time; i.e. that when a magnet acts upon a distant magnet or piece of iron, the influencing cause, (which I may for the moment call magnetism,) proceeds gradually from the magnetic bodies, and requires time for its transmission, which will probably be found to be very sensible.

I think also, that I see reason for supposing that electric induction (of tension) is also performed in a similar progressive way.

I am inclined to compare the diffusion of magnetic forces from a magnetic pole, to the vibrations upon the surface of disturbed water, or those of air in the phenomena of sound: i.e. I am inclined to think the vibratory theory will apply to these phenomena, as it does to sound, and most probably to light.

By analogy I think it may possibly apply to the phenomena of electricity of tension also.

These views I wish to work out experimentally: but as much of my time is engaged in the duties of my office, and as the experiments will therefore be prolonged, and may in their course be subject to the observation of others; I wish, by depositing this paper in the care of the Royal Society, to take possession as it were of a certain date, and so have right, if they are confirmed by experiments, to claim credit for the views at that date: at which time as far as I know no one is conscious of or can claim them but myself.

M Faraday

Faraday's sealed note deposited with the Royal Society in 1832.

In suggesting that magnetic and electric actions might take time, and in comparing the spread of a magnetic field to the spreading of a sound wave, Faraday was introducing radical new ideas. These new ideas were not accepted at first, probably partly at least because they were not understood. The first person to treat the new ideas seriously was William Thomson (later Lord Kelvin, the first person to be raised to the peerage in recognition of his scientific achievements). In 1845 he showed how the lines of force could be treated mathematically.

A few years later Faraday's speculations caught the imagination of a young mathematician at Cambridge, James Clerk Maxwell. He wanted to pursue research in electrical theory and, after consulting Thomson Maxwell set out to develop Faraday's ideas in mathematical form. He wrote to Faraday:

you are the first person in whom the idea of bodies acting at a distance by throwing the surrounding medium into a state of constraint has arisen, as a principle to be actually believed in ... nothing is clearer than your description of all sources of force keeping up a state of energy in all that surrounds them.

Faraday's reservations about mathematics and lack of mathematical skill himself have been noted, but he was impressed by Maxwell's work even though he could not follow all the argument. In 1857 Faraday wrote to Maxwell: 'I was at first almost frightened when I saw such mathematical force made to bear upon the subject, and then wondered to see that the subject stood it so well'. He added that he hoped to undertake experiments on the time of magnetic action, speculating that the 'time must probably be short as the time of light'. At that date neither man appears to have suggested that light itself was an electromagnetic phenomenon, but their thoughts must have been moving that way, and it was late in 1861 that Maxwell stated the view firmly, first in a letter to Faraday and then to William Thomson.

FIELDS

The impact of Maxwell's mathematical development of Faraday's ideas was such that many of the physicists who followed him in the theoretical study of electromagnetism were known as 'Maxwellians'.

Maxwell's work led to the conclusion that there must be electromagnetic waves which could travel through space with the speed of light. The great achievement of the German physicist Heinrich Hertz (1857-1894) was to demonstrate that the prediction was right. With quite simple equipment Hertz managed to produce electromagnetic waves and then detect them a short distance away.

In Paris Edouard Branly found that a tube of metal filings changed its electrical resistance in the presence of electromagnetic waves. This arrangement, which was called the 'coherer', because the metal particles 'cohered' together, offered a sensitive detector of electromagnetic waves.

Practical radio is due to the Irish-Italian Guglielmo Marconi, who transmitted signals over a distance of one kilometre in Bolgna. Then in 1896, he began a series of experiments with the British Post Office. Radio was first used for point-to-point communication. The idea of broadcasting to the public generally, for information and entertainment, soon followed. Once sound broadcasting was established the idea of television was a natural development, but the initial broadcasts were brought to an abrupt stop by the outbreak of war in 1939. The war, however, stimulated another application of electromagnetic waves. The waves can be reflected by metal objects and the reflections of the waves by ships or aircraft is the basis of radar.

The most recent application of electromagnetic waves is one that could not possibly have occurred to Maxwell, Hertz or Marconi. High frequency electromagnetic waves carry energy which is converted into heat when the waves reach an electrically conducting object, but they do not heat the air in between. That is the basis of the microwave cooker.

THE PUBLIC FIGURE

Back in 1835, after several years of continuous hard work, Faraday was in need of a holiday. He made a tour of Switzerland, during which he renewed his friendship with the Swiss scientist Auguste de la Rive (1801-1873) whom he had met, together with his father Gaspard (1770-1834), on the Continental tour with Davy. He then returned to the Royal Institution to carry on his research work, but by 1838 his health was failing and he had to do less work.

In 1841 he needed a complete rest. He left the Royal Institution for eight months during which he again went to Switzerland with his wife and her brother. For the rest of his life he suffered loss of memory and attacks of giddiness, though his physical health was mostly good. During the winter of 1849-50 he was troubled by a persistent sore throat which prevented him from lecturing. The trouble was traced to some bad teeth which were later extracted. Michael Faraday's account of going to the dentist shows how fair-minded he was, even in a matter which had brought him great pain: 'Because of much pain in my jaw and the known bad state of my teeth ..... I went on Monday morning to the dentist. He pulled out five teeth and a fang. He had much trouble and I much pain..... On the whole the operation was well and cleverly carried on by the dentist, the fault was in the teeth.'

His later work was a series of short bursts of activity rather than the long periods of intensive research which had filled his earlier years. His memory often failed him when he tried to recall recent events, but he could remember events of long before, including the unfortunate incident in 1821 when he was suspected of stealing Wollaston's ideas. He was reluctant to begin research into subject on which other people were working, in case the same thing happened again. Throughout his life Faraday displayed no interest in politics of any kind. He remarked to his friend Auguste de la Rive 'For me, who never meddle with politics and who think very little of them as one of the games of life, it seems sad that Scientific men should be so disturbed by them'. He was, however, a loyal subject of the Queen and his services were always available when his advice was sought by the government on scientific matters.Much of his time was now spent on advising the Government and other public bodies on scientific matters.

Faraday had become a public figure whose advice was sought by the Government on important scientific matters. For many years he had declined to act as a consultant because he wanted to spend all his time and energy on research. One of his last pieces of consultancy had been in 1832 for the

Admiralty, when he analysed some samples of oatmeal which were suspected of being adulterated. Now that his health stopped him doing continuous research, his talents were again available to the Government.

In 1844 there was a public outcry about the safety of coal mines after ninety-five miners were killed in an explosion at Haswell Colliery in County Durham. The Prime Minister, Sir Robert Peel, decided that a chemist and a geologist should make an inquiry into the accident to find the cause and recommend ways of avoiding similar accidents in future. Faraday and Sir Charles Lyell were chosen and travelled to Durham to hold their inquiry. They found that it was possible to light a pipe from a Davy safety lamp, and that although smoking was strictly forbidden there had been cases of men smoking in the mine.

Lyell noticed with surprise how Faraday changed from a scientific investigator into an able cross-examiner. Faraday had taken a keen interest in the question of the reliability of evidence. In one of his notebooks he compared the values of evidence and argument: 'Testimony is like an arrow shot from a longbow; the force of it depends on the strength of the hand that draws it. Argument is like an arrow shot from a crossbow, which has equal force though shot by a child.'

During the inquiry Faraday asked one of the mine inspectors how they measured the rate at which air flowed through the mine. The inspector showed how it was done. He took a pinch of gunpowder in one hand and a lighted candle in the other. The gunpowder was allowed to fall through the candle flame, and an assistant with a watch noted how long the smoke took to travel a certain distance. Faraday asked where the gunpowder was kept. The inspector seemed reluctant to tell him, but said it was kept in a bag whose neck was tied up. 'But where do you keep the bag?' demanded Faraday. 'You are sitting on it,' came the reply. It was the most comfortable seat available, so they had given it to Faraday!

Faraday was one of a committee set up in 1850 to look into the problem of preserving the paintings in the National Gallery. London in those days was a dirty, smoky city, and the combined effects of dirt in the air and the close presence of thousands of visitors every day was wreaking havoc on the pictures. The committee recommended that all the pictures should be covered with glass, and this was done. It was appreciated that this was not a complete solution to the problem, and Faraday made a study of the chemistry of varnishes for covering pictures.

Later he was consulted about the famous Elgin marbles at the British Museum. He found, however, that nothing could be done to restore the marbles to their original condition, though he suggested ways of stopping further deterioration.

For nearly thirty years, until 1851, Faraday lectured in chemistry at the Royal Military Academy at Woolwich.

From 1836 he was a Scientific Adviser to Trinity House, the body responsible for lighthouses around the British coast. There is little record of his work for Trinity House until the later 1850s, because the box of papers and reports on lighthouses which he left to Trinity House at his death was destroyed during the Second World War. In 1860, however, he summarised his duties in a report that was published in the report to Parliament of the 'Commissioners appointed to enquire into the conditions and management of lights, buoys and beacons'.

In 1836 I was appointed 'Scientific advisor to the Corporation of the Trinity House in experiments on Lights.' Since then a large part of my attention has been given to the lighthouses in respect of their ventilation, their lightning conductors and arrangements, the impurity and cure of water, the provision of domestic water, the examination of optical apparatus, etc., the results of which may be seen in various reports to the Trinity House. A very large part also of my consideration has been given to the numerous propositions of all kinds which have been and are presented continually to the Corporation; few of these present any reasonable prospect of practical and useful application, and I have been obliged to use my judgement, chiefly in checking imperfect and unsafe propositions, rather than in forwarding any which could be advanced to a practical result.

Extract from Faraday's account of his Lighthouse duties.

One of the proposed new lights on which he reported was a limelight, in which a flame of hydrogen burning in oxygen heated a piece of lime to produce a brilliant light. The system undoubtedly worked and produced a good light, but Faraday doubted whether the gases could be produced reliably in the conditions of a lighthouse. Much more promising, in Faraday's view, was the electric arc, and in particular the arc lamp designed by Professor Holmes. He expressed the hope that a situation could be selected where the lamp could tried 'for a time and under circumstances during which all the liabilities may be thoroughly eliminated. The light is so intense, so abundant, so concentrated and focal, so free from under shadow (caused in the common lamp by the burner), so free from flickering, that one cannot but desire that it should succeed'. But he appreciated that it would have to be introduced carefully and gradually, and men trained to operate it.

Faraday's recommendation that Holmes' scheme should be tried out in practice was put into effect at the South Foreland Lighthouse. His report to Trinity House was not only concerned with the question of whether Holmes' light would work, but it also considered the cost of running the steam engine which drove the generator and the higher wages that would have to be paid for skilled men to operate the new equipment. When any new idea was being tried out in a lighthouse, someone had to check that all was well. Even when he was seventy years old, Faraday still made occasional visits on behalf of Trinity House. In one report written in

23 Holmes' generator for supplying an arc lamp in a lighthouse.

1860 he explained that he had tried to visit a lighthouse in Kent but the road was

blocked by snow. When he returned a few days later, the road was still blocked, but he managed to cross walls, hedges and fields to reach the lighthouse and finish his duties.

This was clearly work for someone younger. He continued as Scientific Advisor until 1865, by which time neither his mind nor his body could stand the strain. In May 1865 he made his last report for Trinity House and then retired, being followed in the post by John Tyndall who also succeeded him at the Royal Institution.

In 1862 Faraday gave evidence to the Public Schools Commission. This was a Royal Commission set up with the Earl of Clarendon as chairman to investigate the education given in the Public Schools. Faraday drew the Commissioners' attention to the complete lack of science teaching in the Public Schools. He complained that people who had received the traditional Public School education

24 John Tyndall.

based on the classics were ignorant of natural science and, what made it worse, they did not realise that they were ignorant. Faraday was asked whether science could be taught in such a way that examinations could be set to test the pupils. He was sure it was possible. He drew attention to the enthusiasm of schoolboys and girls who attended his lectures, and stressed the need for good teaching.

Apart from his own lifetime's experience of lecturing on scientific subjects, Faraday could also speak from his experience as a Senator of the University of London. The University had been established in 1836 as an examining body, not a teaching one, and one of the honours which gave Faraday most pleasure was his appointment by the Crown as one of the first members of the Senate.

RETIREMENT

By 1861 Faraday knew that he could no longer carry out all his duties, especially the Juvenile Lectures for which he felt a clear and ordered mind was particularly essential. His letter of resignation includes his own account of how he first came to the Institution and how he felt about his work there.

To the Managers of the Royal Institution,

It is with the deepest feeling that I address you. I entered the Royal Institution in March 1813, nearly forty-nine years ago, and, with the exception of a comparatively short period, during which I was abroad on the Continent with Sir H. Davy, have been with you ever since. During that time I have been most happy in your kindness, and in the fostering care which the Royal Institution has bestowed upon me. Thank God, first, for all his gifts. I have next to thank you and your predecessors for the unswerving encouragement and support which you have given me during that period. My life has been a happy one, and all that I desired. During its progress I have tried to make a fitting return for it to the Royal Institution, and through it to science. But the progress of years (now amounting in number to threescore and ten) having brought forth first the period of development, and then that of maturity, have ultimately produced for me that of gentle decay. This has taken place in such a manner as to make the evening of life a blessing; for whilst increasing physical weakness occurs, a full share of health free from pain is granted with it; and whilst memory and certain other faculties of the mind diminish, my good spirits and cheerfulness do not diminish with them.

Still I am not able to do as I have done....

The managers accepted his resignation as lecturer, but asked him to stay as Superintendent of the house and laboratories. These remaining duties he resigned in 1865, so ending all his connection with the Royal Institution. The feeling of the members towards him was such that the previous year he had been offered the Presidency of the Institution, but he declined because he knew he was no longer able to carry out the duties of this office.

At Prince Albert's suggestion the Queen offered Faraday a Grace and Favour Residence, a house at Hampton Court, in 1858 for the rest of his life. Prince Albert, Queen Victoria's consort, was interested in scientific matters and was largely responsible for the Great Exhibition of 1851. He had a high regard for Faraday, and took his son, the Prince of Wales (later Edward VII), to hear him lecture. A painting of the scene by Alexander Blaikley now hangs in the Institution. Faraday himself was invited to Windsor Castle to discuss science with Prince Albert. Faraday hesitated to accept the offer at first, for fear that he could not afford the cost of certain repairs. When this came to the Queen's ears she arranged for the repairs to be done at her own expense, and Faraday gladly accepted the house. Until 1862 he still spent most of his time at the Royal Institution, but thereafter Hampton Court became his home.

In his last years, Michael Faraday gradually became weaker, and died peacefully sitting in his armchair at Hampton Court on 25 August 1867. By his own wish the funeral was private and simple, and the stone on his grave in Highgate cemetery recorded simply his name and the dates of his birth and death.

* * *

Many tributes have been paid to Faraday since his death. More than twenty books have been written about him. The centenary of his discovery of electromagnetic induction, the most significant of all his discoveries, was celebrated in 1931 with an exhibition in the Royal Albert Hall, London. The bicentenary of his birth is being marked in 1991 by exhibitions, conferences and lectures. The Post Office is issuing a commemorative postage stamp. The Bank of England is putting Faraday's portrait on a newly designed £20 note. That is quite an achievement for the blacksmith's son who saw books on science and became fascinated by what he read.

Faraday's scientific life was devoted to finding out how the physical world worked, and to explaining science to the public. He was not himself interested in developing new inventions from his discoveries, though he was happy for other people to do so. In 1891, on the centenary of his birth, the magazine *Punch* published a cartoon showing Faraday using a phonograph, which was then one of the latest scientific wonders. A map in the background shows telegraph cables around the world, and a telephone. No electric light is shown, although electric lighting was becoming common by that date. The cartoonist shows Faraday impressed by the advances of science in the twenty-four years from his death. How much more would he be surprised to see developments after a further hundred years.

25 Faraday (returned): "Well, Miss Science, I heartily congratulate you; you have made Marvellous Progress since my Time!"

FOR FURTHER READING

There are many biographies of Faraday, and accounts of aspects of his work. For a comprehensive, full-length biography see L Pearce Williams: *Michael Faraday: a biography*, 1967.

Recent studies of aspects of Faraday's life and work will be found in David Gooding and Frank A J L James (Eds): *Faraday Rediscovered - Essays on the Life and Work of Michael Faraday, 1791-1867*, Macmillan 1985

Faraday's Journal written during the visit to Europe with Sir Humphry Davy is published in Brian Bowers and Lenore Symons (Eds): *Curiosity Perfectly Satisfyed: Faraday's travels in Europe 1813-1815*, Peter Peregrinus Ltd, 1991.

Readers of this book may also be interested in the IEE Faraday Lecture which is sponsored in the bicentenary year (1991) by Philips Electronics and Imperial College. (Details of the lecture tour, and tickets, are available from the Faraday Officer, Institution of Electrical Engineers, Savoy Place, London, WC2R 0BL).